Help Me Be Good

Being Mean

Joy Berry
Illustrated by Bartholomew

Joy Berry Books
New York

This is Robbie and Katie. Reading about Robbie and Katie can help you understand why people are sometimes mean. It can also help you avoid being mean to others.

If you do something on purpose to hurt anotherperson, you are being mean. When you are being mean to someone, you intentionally hurt the person's body, feelings, or belongings.

Sometimes people are mean because they want attention. They want to be noticed.

Being mean will not get you the kind of attention you want or need.

Try not to be mean when you need or want attention. Instead, tell someone in a kind way that you need attention. Ask the person to spend some time with you.

Sometimes people are mean because they don't know a better way to be funny. They want to make themselves or other people laugh.

Doing something that hurts someone or damagessomething is never funny. Being mean is never funny!

Try not to be mean when you want to be funny. Before you do something you think is funny to another person, be certain that the person will agree that what you are doing is funny.

Make surethe person will not be hurt in any way, and that no one's belongings will be damaged.

Some people are mean because they feel angry or frustrated and don't know a better way to express their anger or frustration.

Being mean is not a good way to express anger or frustration. Being mean often creates situations that will make you feel even more angry or frustrated.

Try not to express your anger or frustration by being mean. It is OK to express your anger or frustration by crying, yelling, jumping up and down,or hitting something that cannot be damaged, such as a pillow, punching bag, or bed. To avoid bothering anyone, you might need to go outside or into a room by yourself and close the door.

Some people are mean because they have been hurt and they want to get back at someone. These people try to make themselves feel better by hurting the person who has hurt them or hurting someone else.

Getting back at someone is not a good way to make yourself feel better when you are hurt. Getting back at someone might make the person want to get back at you, fand you might get hurt again.

Try not to be mean when you have been hurt.
Instead, talk to the person who has hurt you.
Let the person know that you have been hurt
and that you feel bad about whatever happened.

Stay away from the person who has hurt you
until you are certain that he or she will not hurt
you again.

It is important to treat other people the way you want to be treated. If you don't want other people to be mean to you, you should not be mean to them.

Joy Berry Enterprises
146 West 29th St., Suite 11RW
New York, NY 10001

Cover Design & Art Direction: John Bellaud
Cover Illustration & Art Production: Geoff Glisson

Production Location: HX Printing, Guangzhou, China
Date of Production: July 2010
Cohort: Batch 1

Printed in China
ISBN 978-1-60577-142-7